HAPPY FATHER'S DAY, DAD!

CELEBRATIONS FROM AROUND THE WORLD
THE HOLIDAY BOOK FOR KINDERGARTEN
CHILDREN'S HOLIDAY BOOKS

Speedy Publishing LLC

40 E. Main St. #1156

Newark, DE 19711

www.speedypublishing.com

Copyright 2017

Fathers are pretty wonderful! Fathers and mothers together raise their children and make a good home. Just as we honor mothers on Mother's Day each year, on a different day we take time to show our fathers how we love and appreciate them. Let's find out more about Father's Day around the world.

Happy
Father's
Day
THANK YOU DADDY!

THE START OF FATHER'S DAY

Honoring our fathers is not a new thing. In fact, historians found a Father's Day card that was made four thousand years ago in Babylon! A boy named Elmesu made a card out of clay with a message for his father: he wished his dad long life and good health.

owever, until recent times there was not a regular event each year to celebrate fathers. Then a woman named Sonora Smart Dodd was sitting in a church in Spokane, Washington on Mother's Day in 1909. As she listened to a sermon about how great mothers are and how much hard work they do, she started to think about her father.

SONORA SMART DODD

He had raised six children on his own after his wife died. Sonora Dodd started to think, "Why is there not a day for fathers?"

She organized the first Father's Day for the very next year, 1910, in Spokane. But it took her years of campaigning to get Father's Day recognized as a national event.

FIRST FATHER'S DAY IN SPOKANE

In 1916, President Woodrow Wilson approved the idea of such a holiday, and in 1924 President Calvin Coolidge made Father's Day an annual event in the United States.

PRESIDENT RICHARD NIXON
WITH HIS DAUGHTERS

For a long time Father's Day did not happen on a fixed date or on a fixed schedule. Finally, in 1972, President Richard Nixon signed a law fixing the third Sunday in June as the annual day for Father's Day.

Daddy

WHAT HAPPENS ON FATHER'S DAY

In the United States, about three quarters of the population celebrates Father's Day, although they may do very different things on that day. A lot of people send or give cards on the day. Half of the cards are sent by children to their fathers or grandfathers, and about one card in five is sent by a wife to her husband.

Beyond the sending of cards, there are very different ways to make dad feel good on Father's Day.

Gifts: Many people give dad something that they hope he will like and enjoy, something he might not get around to buying for himself. Gifts can range from food to neckties, from books to concert tickets; but of course the thing all gifts have in common is that they carry love from the giver to the receiver of the gift.

WRAPPED GIFT FOR DAD

HAPPY
FATHER'S
DAY

Roses: We may think that flowers and Mother's Day go together, but there is also a tradition of giving dads roses on Father's Day. In some cases this may involve planting a new rose bush that will last for years, rather than presenting a bouquet of flowers that will last a few days.

Events: In many families, Father's Day is a good excuse to go to a special sporting event, concert, or other activity that not just dad, but many members of the family can enjoy.

FAMILY PARTICIPATING IN THE COLOR RUN EVENT

Special treatment: Maybe we bring dad breakfast in bed. Maybe we wash his car or mow the lawn when it's not our turn.

Any special effort to make Dad feel special is a good gift to honor the spirit of the day.

Listening: On Father's Day, why not ask your dad to tell you a story about when he was young, or about when the family was first starting, before you were born?

Perhaps he has a story to tell about how he almost lost his first job, or what he learned from his own dad. Stories are precious: you give the gift of listening to your father, and get a gift of understanding back from him.

DONATE CLOTHES

Donations: Maybe Dad already has a lot of cool stuff, from tools to toys. Maybe what he would really understand as a gift would be a donation in his name to a good cause that he cares about. The good cause would differ from father to father, because all dads have different interests, so thinking a little bit about what your dad or grandfather finds important can help lead you to the right sort of donation to make in his honor.

People in Canada do many of the same things that people in the United States do to honor the dads in the family. Often Father's Day in Canada is when families hold reunions and kids who live most of the year far away come home for the special day. Restaurants in both Canada and the U.S. report a lot of business on Father's Day, as families take Dad out for a special breakfast, lunch, or dinner.

In the **United Kingdom**, **Ireland**, and **Australia**, schools and community organizations organize events for Father's Day. These events highlight how important fathers are in the national culture.

They are also a great thing for fathers whose families are no longer available, and who would otherwise have no celebration they could take part in.

FAMILY HAVING PICNIC

In South Africa, Father's Day is often a special chance to have a picnic or go on a fishing trip with Dad.

Father's Day in **Thailand** is also the king's birthday. The day is marked with firework displays and by people performing good deeds. Two good deeds that many Thais try to do on the day are donating blood and freeing animals that are in captivity.

GRAND PALACE AT TWILIGHT IN BANGKOK, THAILAND

FAMILY CELEBRATING FATHER'S DAY

Father's Day as a celebration is new in **India**. Not a lot of families celebrate the holiday, as it is less than ten years old. Families in cities, which may have heard of how Father's Day is held in the United States, are more likely to observe it in India than families that live in more isolated areas of the country.

FATHER'S DAY AROUND THE WORLD

Most countries around the world now have holidays to honor fathers, but they do not all fall on the same day of the year. Here are the dates of some national celebrations:

March 19 (St. Joseph's Day)

Portugal, Spain, Belgium (Belgium also celebrates fathers on the second Sunday in June)

ST. JOSEPH'S DAY AND
FATHER'S DAY CELEBRATIONS

First Sunday in June:

Lithuania

June 20:

Bulgaria

Third Sunday in June:

Argentina, Chile, Canada, France, India, Japan, the Netherlands, the United Kingdom, the United States

August 8:

Taiwan

Second Sunday in August:

Brazil

First Sunday in September:
Australia, New Zealand, Sweden

Second Sunday in November:

Denmark, Finland, Norway

NORWEGIAN FAMILY CELEBRATING FATHER'S DAY

Forty days after Easter (Ascension Day):

Germany

GERMAN FAMILY CELEBRATING FATHER'S DAY

December 5 (King's birthday):

Thailand

KEEPING THE DAY ABOUT DAD

The main thing to remember is that this special day is not about how big a party you can throw, or how much money you can spend on a gift or a card. It's about remembering how much all the dads in our society do to make families and the whole nation stronger and happier.

Here are some cool Dad facts:

- More than half of all children are praised as much as three times a day by their father.

- In the United States there are about 65 million fathers with young children living in their homes.

- About 14 percent of fathers stay home and take care of the house and the children, while the mother goes to work and makes money for the family.

- In families where the dad works and the mom stays home to take care of the kids, almost one third of fathers say they would be happy to find a job that made less money if it let them spend more time with their family.

- Most children in families who are under six years old, eat the main meal of almost every day with their father.

HALSEY TAYLOR

- Halsey Taylor's father died in 1896 from drinking water that was not clean. Halsey invented several designs for public drinking fountains that would deliver safe and healthy water for anyone who needed a drink, so other children would not suffer the same sort of loss he had suffered.

THE WASHINGTON FAMILY

- George Washington, the first President of the United States, is sometimes called "The Father of His Country". But he had no children of his own, apart from two he adopted.

- Cosmonaut Yuri Usachev of Russia was commanding the International Space Station on Father's Day, 2001. The technology company RadioShack put together a talking picture frame, which was a new thing at that time. Usachev's daughter recorded a message and the picture frame was secretly sent to the space station with other supplies. Usachev got a wonderful surprise gift on Father's Day.

- Among fish, the female seahorse lays a couple's eggs. But it is the male seahorse who protects and takes care of the eggs until the babies are born.

- Dick Hoyt had a son, Rick, who had a severe illness, cerebral palsy. Dick pushed his son's wheelchair, with Rick aboard, through hundreds of marathon races to give his son the experience of competitive running. Rick cannot speak, but he can communicate using a special computer. He has told his dad that, when they are in a race together, Rick often forgets that he is disabled.

DICK HOYT AND HIS SON

HOLIDAYS, HOLIDAYS, HOLIDAYS!

Every culture has holidays to celebrate people, seasons, and great historical events. Learn about some of them in Baby Professor books like *Why do the Chinese have a Different New Year?*, *Who Started the Labor Day Celebration?*, and *Why do we Celebrate Halloween?*

ATHER'S
Y

Visit

BABY PROFESSOR
EDUCATION KIDS

www.BabyProfessorBooks.com

to download Free Baby Professor eBooks and view
our catalog of new and exciting Children's Books